KETO DIET COOKBOOK FOR BEGINNERS

by Kristine Hogan

Table of Contents

Introduction

I've been overweight all my life. However, I never thought too much about my weight and appearance. I've never been interested in beauty standards, fashion, and trends. Growing up, I realized that I am smart enough to learn how to love my body regardless of a socially preferred image. I learned to make many diet-derailing excuses for my unhealthy weight such as "I do not carry about bad beauty trends."; "Life is too short to spend on diets." Unfortunately, I forgot a fundamental thing – my health. I've never had a strong motivation to make a change in my life as long as I realized that I endanger my health. Ultimately, the most disease begins in the gut.

First and foremost, I experienced a burning and sharp back pain; as time went on, it has gotten worse. Plus, I was prediabetic according to my glucose levels. I started a diet, lost some pounds, and then I was bitterly disappointed with my results... I experienced the problem that many of us face, the so-called yo-yo effect! Extreme calorie restriction can disrupt hormones that control appetite and satiety; plus, the amount of leptin in our body can drastically drop (leptin is produced by fat cells), so our body tends to refill its fat cells. Consequently, it increases our appetite. One day, I stumbled upon the concept of healthy eating that is based on protein foods and fats, with zero to low-carb foods. It means weight loss without dieting! I was very skeptical, but that concept intrigued me and I decided to learn more about the ketogenic lifestyle. I decided to give it a try, and... Voilà! I lost seven pounds in the first month. Keeping track of calories and carb intake, focusing on protein and healthy fats may sound intimidating; however, if you make health your primary focus in life, you'll succeed. I started cooking regularly for my family and eating at home as much as possible. That's where I found inspiration for this cookbook. I created this recipe collection to help you stop with perpetual dieting and prevent some serious health conditions.

What is so Fascinating about the Ketogenic Diet?

The ketogenic diet is a high-fat, moderate-protein, and low-carb dietary regimen. Your goal should be to get 70 to 75 percent of your daily calories from fat and about 20 to 25 percent from protein; you should limit your total carbohydrate consumption to 35 grams or fewer per day.

Long story short, this diet excludes sugar and promotes healthy fats and protein-based foods. It sounds like a type of diet human beings ate for thousands of years, right? This type of diet promotes real, single-ingredient foods, and a high-quality source of nutrients. The real food is unprocessed; this diet excludes processed foods such as ready-to-eat meals, snacks, packaged foods, canned goods, and so forth. Processed foods are often loaded with sugar, salt, and trans-fats; moreover, these foods, almost without exception, contain artificial flavors colors, and other chemicals that can have devastating effects on human health. With this in mind, I am ready to roll up my sleeves and cook my meals from scratch instead of relying on pre-made versions. Not to mention the pride of putting my masterpiece on the table! To sum up, opt for organic and local foods as much as possible. Focus on whole, seasonal foods that haven't been artificially created.

Foods to avoid on the ketogenic diet include grains and grain-like seeds, common types of flours, rice, legumes (beans, lentils, peas), starchy vegetables (potatoes, sweet potatoes, yams, parsnip), fruits (other than berries), and especially starchy fruits (e.g. banana and plantain), sugars syrups, and sugary drinks. Trans fats and hydrogenated oil are off-limits, too. This includes vegetable shortening, corn oil, soybean oil, and margarine. You can find these harmful fats in processed foods and fast food.

Whether you are following a keto diet, or you're considering this dietary regimen, I created the food list to make your keto grocery shopping easy and manageable.

Meat and Poultry – pork, beef, veal, lamb, goat, chicken, turkey, duck, and goose.

Fish & Seafood – fat fish, white fish, shrimp, mussels, clams, oysters, sea scallops, lobster, crab, and squid.

Dairy products and Eggs – full-fat cheese, sour cream, Greek-style yogurt, cheese, heavy whipping cream, and double cream.

Nuts – almonds, coconut, walnuts, hazelnuts, pecans, pine nuts, peanuts, macadamia nuts, and unsweetened nut butter (preferably homemade versions).

Seeds – Chia seeds, pumpkin seeds (pepitas), hemp seeds, sesame seeds, flax seeds, sunflower seeds, and unsweetened seed kinds of butter such as tahini.

Vegetables – cauliflower broccoli, tomatoes, Brussels sprouts, asparagus, onion, garlic, zucchini, and cucumber. As for the pickled vegetables, make your homemade recipes or pay attention to added sugar.

Healthy fats – olive oil, coconut oil, butter, ghee, and avocado.

Fruits – berries, lemon, and lime.

Herbs and spices – fresh or dried.

Baking ingredients – almond flour, coconut flour, baking powder, baking soda, sugar-free baker's chocolate, and unsweetened cocoa powder.

Sauces & Condiments – vinegar, hot sauce, mustard, tomato sauce, and mayonnaise (no added sugar).

Drinks & Alcoholic beverages – coffee, tea, keto smoothies, zero carb energy drinks, sparkling water, whiskey, brandy, vodka, rum, tequila, and dry wine.

Keto Sweeteners: Stevia and Monk fruit are zero-carb sweeteners; Splenda contains 0.5 grams of carbs per 1 gram while Erythritol and Xylitol both contain 4 grams of carbs per 1 teaspoon.

If you are following a vegan or vegetarian diet, keto-friendly foods include tofu, tempeh, unsweetened, plant-based dairy products, Shirataki noodles, nutritional yeast, and seaweed.

5 Science-Based Health Benefits of the Ketogenic Diet

There are lots of benefits of the ketogenic diet. However, it's important to consult a doctor before starting any sort of diet.

Neuroprotective benefits. Clinical trials have proven that a keto diet can protect your mental health. It can prevent mental diseases like Alzheimer's, Parkinson's, and dementia. It can also cure epilepsy in children.

It reduces insulin levels. Did you know that high blood insulin can lead to serious health issues? A keto diet can be very effective for lowering blood sugar and insulin levels. Consuming low-carb foods has been shown to increase insulin sensitivity. In many studies, a high intake of sugar has been shown to promote insulin resistance.

Blood pressure tends to drop significantly. In another study, a constant intake of low-carb foods has been shown to promote healthy blood pressure. Plus, lowering your carb intake can reduce the risk of heart disease and stroke.

Ideal weight. According to statistics, nearly one-third of the population suffers from obesity. Firth things first, you should boost your metabolism. However, it does not happen overnight. It takes about four weeks to feel the first benefits of a keto diet, so be patient and stay positive. Pay attention to the hidden carbs that can sabotage your diet. Chicken wings with sauce, dairy products, sausage, canned fish, and condiments may contain hidden carbs. Keep an eye on your favorite low-carb foods and condiments when you dine out. Consequently, focus on home-cooked meals since it can lower the risk of obesity and depression.

When it comes to healthy weight loss, you should drink plenty of water on the ketogenic diet. Studies have found that drinking about eight cups of cold water a day can boost your metabolism so you can lose up to 5 pounds in a year. Increase your physical activity; it can help you boost your metabolism, protect your immune system, and lose pounds. You can take the stairs, clean your house, do yoga, and go for a walk as often as possible. Last but not least, use a food tracker app to calculate your net carbs.

It reduces the risk of cancer. Many studies in animals and humans have found that consuming refined carbs can lead to serious health problems. Thus, a diet high in nutrient-rich foods like vegetables, healthy fats, and lean protein may provide some protection against malignant diseases. Following a healthy eating pattern is the key component to overall health and longevity. It includes:

- Food high in vitamins, minerals, and other nutrients;
- Fiber-rich food;
- A colorful variety of veggies;
- Limit your use of sauces, dressings, red meat, and processed meat such as ham, bacon, and hot dogs.

A Few Words About This Recipe Collection

In real life, a healthy lifestyle is a challenging goal. This cookbook can help you kick-start your keto journey and more importantly – stay on track! Throughout this cookbook, you'll find my all-time keto favorites, mouth-watering recipes that can be assembled at any time of the day. From breakfast to snacks, side dishes, and desserts, you'll learn how to prepare the best keto recipes in an easy and creative way. The ketogenic diet constantly inspires me, so I hope it will inspire you as well. All fifty recipes come from home cooks – my grandma, my mom, and my aunt. You will find both traditional and trendy recipes so anybody won't resist a bowl of hearty keto stew or a piece of delectable chocolate cake. Every recipe in this collection includes a suggested number of servings, approximate cooking time, ingredient list, detailed directions, and nutritional analysis.

Do you need healthy and delicious recipes for one of the most popular diets in the world? Well, you are in the right place. The point of this cookbook is to get the most enjoyment and fun out of the ketogenic diet! Let's get cooking!

Breakfast

1. Breakfast Egg Salad

Ingredients

- 6 medium eggs
- 2 ounces bacon bits
- 1/4 cup mayonnaise
- 2 tablespoons cream cheese
- 1 tablespoon fresh lime juice
- 1 scallion stalks chopped
- 1/4 teaspoon dried dill weed
- 1/2 teaspoon cayenne pepper
- Kosher salt and freshly ground black pepper, to taste
- 1 avocado, peeled, pitted and diced
- 1 cup baby spinach

4 Servings   25 minutes

Directions

Add the eggs and water (1-inch above the eggs) to a saucepan and bring to a boil. Remove from the heat and let it sit for 15 minutes.

Peel the eggs and coarsely chop them.

Add in the other ingredients and gently stir to combine. Place the salad in your refrigerator until ready to serve.

Enjoy!

Nutritional Information

Calories: 354; Fat: 32.1g; Carbs: 6.1g; Protein: 11.8g; Sugars: 1.2g; Fiber: 3.6g

2. Bacon and Spinach Frittata

Ingredients

- 2 tablespoons butter
- 1 teaspoon garlic, crushed
- 1 tablespoon scallions, chopped
- 6 large eggs
- 1/3 cup heavy cream
- 2 ounces bacon bits
- 1 cup brown mushrooms, sliced
- 1 cup baby spinach
- 1 cup Monterey-Jack cheese, shredded
- 1/2 teaspoon red pepper flakes, crushed
- Sea salt and ground black pepper, to taste

4 Servings   **35 minutes**

Directions

Grease a baking pan with 1 tablespoon of butter.

Melt the remaining 1 tablespoon of butter in a frying pan over medium-high heat. Sauté the garlic and scallions for about 30 seconds or until just tender and aromatic.

In a bowl, whisk the eggs until frothy; fold in the other ingredients. Spoon the egg mixture into the baking pan.

Bake in the preheated oven at 360 degrees F for 30 minutes or until the eggs do not jiggle in the middle. Devour!

Nutritional Information

Calories: 386; Fat: 32.2g; Carbs: 3.7g; Protein: 20.5g; Sugars: 1.8g; Fiber: 0.6g

3. Mexican Breakfast Tacos

Ingredients

- 2 tablespoons full-fat milk
- 2 eggs
- 2 cups Cheddar cheese, shredded
- 1 tablespoon Taco seasoning blend
- 1/2 cup sour cream
- 1 medium avocado, peeled, pitted and diced
- 1 cup iceberg lettuce

4 Servings   15 minutes

Directions

Whisk the milk and eggs until frothy and pale.

Fold in the cheese and Taco seasoning blend; mix to combine well.

Preheat your oven to 350 degrees F. Line a baking sheet with a parchment paper. Bake the cheese taco shells for about 6 minutes or until the edges of the cheese are brown.

Add your toppings and enjoy!

Nutritional Information

Calories: 394; Fat: 32.1g; Carbs: 9.4g; Protein: 18.5g; Sugars: 1.6g; Fiber: 3.9g

4. Deviled Eggs with Bacon

Ingredients

- 2 ounces bacon, chopped
- 8 large eggs
- 4 tablespoons cream cheese
- 4 tablespoons mayonnaise
- 1 tablespoon freshly-squeezed lemon juice
- 1 teaspoon Dijon mustard
- 1/2 teaspoon garlic, crushed
- Sea salt and freshly cracked black pepper, to taste

4 Servings   **15 minutes**

Directions

Cook the bacon in a nonstick skillet over a medium-high flame; reserve.

Cook the eggs in a small saucepan and bring to a boil. Remove from the heat and let it stand, covered, for about 10 minutes.

Then, peel the eggs and separate the egg whites and yolks.

Mix the egg yolks with the remaining ingredients, including the reserved bacon. Divide the filling between the egg whites and serve well-chilled. Devour!

Nutritional Information

Calories: 343; Fat: 29.7g; Carbs: 1.9g; Protein: 15.5g; Sugars: 1.3g; Fiber: 0.1g

5. Classic Eggs in a Mug

Ingredients

- 2 eggs
- 2 tablespoons sour cream
- Sea salt and ground black pepper, to taste
- 1 tablespoon fresh chives, chopped

1 Servings

5 minutes

Directions

Crack the eggs into a microwave-safe mug; mix in the sour cream, salt, and black pepper.

Heat the eggs in your microwave for about 90 seconds until cooked through.

Top your eggs with fresh chives. Bon appétit!

Nutritional Information

Calories: 354; Fat: 32.1g; Carbs: 6.1g; Protein: 11.8g; Sugars: 1.2g; Fiber: 3.6g

6. Breakfast Fat Bombs

Ingredients

- 6 hard-boiled eggs, chopped
- 9 ounces feta cheese
- 2 tablespoons butter
- 2 tablespoons scallions, minced
- 4 ounces pork rinds
- 1 tablespoon sesame seeds

6 Servings

15 minutes

Directions

Mix the eggs, cheese, butter, and scallions.

Roll the mixture into small balls. Roll the balls onto the pork rinds and sesame seeds; place them on a foil-lined baking sheet.

Bon appétit!

Nutritional Information

14

Calories: 313; Fat: 26.7g; Carbs: 2.9g; Protein: 15.5g; Sugars: 2.3g; Fiber: 0.3g

7. Egg and Ham Muffins

Ingredients

- 9 eggs
- 1 scallion stalk, chopped
- 1 garlic clove, minced
- 4 ounces ham, chopped
- Sea salt and ground black pepper, to taste
- 1/2 teaspoon smoked paprika
- 1½ cups Colby cheese, shredded
- 2 tablespoons flaxseed meal
- 1/4 teaspoon baking soda

6 Servings   25 minutes

Directions

Start by preheating your oven to 355 degrees F

Thoroughly combine all of the above ingredients until well mixed.

Coat a muffin pan with cupcake liners. Spoon the batter into the muffin pan. Bake in the preheated oven for about 15 minutes.

Place on a wire rack for 10 minutes before unmolding and serving. Enjoy!

Nutritional Information

Calories: 313; Fat: 26.4g; Carbs: 2.7g; Protein: 15.5g; Sugars: 2.3g; Fiber: 0.3g

Vegetables & Side Dishes

8. Favorite Zucchini Casserole

Ingredients

- 1 pound zucchini, thinly sliced
- 1 large white onion, thinly sliced
- 1/2 teaspoon sea salt
- 1/4 teaspoon ground black pepper
- 1 teaspoon Italian spice mix
- 4 eggs
- 4 garlic cloves, minced
- 1/2 cup cream cheese
- 1 ½ cups Monterey-Jack cheese, shredded
- 1/2 cup parmesan cheese, grated

5 Servings   45 minutes

Directions

Start by preheating your oven to 370 degrees F. Lightly grease a casserole dish with a nonstick cooking spray.

Place 1/2 of the zucchini slices in the dish; place 1/2 of the onion sliced; sprinkle with the spices.

Whisk the eggs until pale and frothy; add in the garlic, cream cheese, and Monterey-Jack cheese. Top the casserole with the cheese mixture. Repeat the layers one more time.

Place the casserole in the preheated oven and bake for about 35 minutes.

Top with Parmesan cheese and place the casserole under the preheated broiler; broil for about 5 minutes or until the edges are nicely browned. Bon appétit!

Nutritional Information

Calories: 349; Fat: 25.7g; Carbs: 9.1g; Protein: 19.7g; Sugars: 2.2g; Fiber: 1.6g

9. Mexican-Style Stuffed Peppers

Ingredients

- 1 tablespoon olive oil
- 1 Spanish onion, chopped
- 1 teaspoon garlic, crushed
- 1 cup tomato puree
- 1 pound ground turkey
- 1 teaspoon Taco seasoning mix
- Kosher salt and ground black pepper, to taste
- 5 bell peppers, deveined
- 1 cup cauliflower, grated
- 1 cup cheddar cheese, shredded

5 Servings

45 minutes

Directions

Heat the olive oil in a saucepan over a moderately high flame. Now, sauté the onion for about 3 minutes or until they are just tender and fragrant.

Then, sauté the garlic for about 30 seconds or until aromatic.

Add a splash of tomato puree and water to deglaze the pan. Add in the ground turkey and seasoning and continue to cook for about 5 minutes or until the meat is no longer pink; reserve.

Add in the cauliflower and remove the pan from the heat.

Stuff the peppers with the turkey mixture; arrange them in a lightly-oiled baking dish. Pour the remaining tomato puree around the stuffed peppers.

Bake the peppers in the preheated oven at 390 degrees F for 30 minutes. Top with cheddar cheese, return to the oven and bake an additional 4 to 5 minutes. Enjoy!

Nutritional Information

Calories: 299; Fat: 17.5g; Carbs: 9g; Protein: 25.3g; Sugars: 4.4g; Fiber: 1.8g

10. Creamy Cheesy Spinach

Ingredients

- 3 tablespoons butter
- 2 garlic, crushed
- 1 scallion stalk, chopped
- 1 pound fresh spinach, roughly chopped
- 1/4 teaspoon dried dill
- 1/2 teaspoon red pepper flakes, crushed
- Kosher salt and ground black pepper, to taste
- 4 eggs, whisked
- 1 cup heavy cream
- 1/2 cup Provolone cheese, grated

4 Servings   25 minutes

Directions

Melt the butter in an oven-proof skillet over medium-high heat. Then, sauté the garlic and scallions for 1 minute or so.

Fold in the spinach leaves, cover and let it simmer for 2 to 3 minutes or until the spinach wilts. Season with dried dill, red pepper, salt, and ground black pepper.

Fold in the eggs, cream and cheese and gently stir until everything is well incorporated.

Place your skillet in the preheated oven at 350 degrees F for about 15 minutes or until the cheese melts.

Bon appétit!

Nutritional Information

Calories: 325; Fat: 28.5g; Carbs: 6.5g; Protein: 14.5g; Sugars: 2.2g; Fiber: 2.8g

11. Easy Eggplant Bake

Ingredients

- 1 pound eggplant, thinly sliced
- 1 teaspoon dried oregano
- 1 teaspoon dried parsley flakes
- Sea salt and ground black pepper, to taste
- 2 tablespoons olive oil
- 2 garlic cloves, minced
- 2 scallion stalks, chopped
- 1 cup tomato purée
- 2 eggs, beaten
- 1 cup sour cream
- 1 cup cheddar cheese, shredded

4 Servings

35 minutes

Directions

Start by preheating your oven to 370 degrees F. Line a baking pan with a piece of parchment paper.

Toss the eggplant rounds with the spices and olive oil; place them on the baking sheet. Bake for 15 minutes, flipping them over halfway through the cooking time.

In the meantime, mix the other ingredients until everything is well combined.

Top the roasted eggplant with the cheese mixture. Continue to bake for 15 minutes more or until the cheese is hot and bubbling.

Bon appétit!

Nutritional Information

Calories: 363; Fat: 27.7g; Carbs: 16g; Protein: 15.4g; Sugars: 6.2g; Fiber: 4.3g

12. The Best Vegetarian Patties Ever

Ingredients

- 1 medium onion, chopped
- 2 cloves garlic, minced
- 8 ounces brown mushrooms, chopped
- 8 ounces cauliflower rice
- 2 tablespoons flax seeds, ground
- 1 teaspoon soy sauce
- 1 teaspoon dried parsley flakes
- Sea salt and ground black pepper, to taste
- 1 teaspoon smoked paprika
- 1/2 teaspoon cumin
- 1 cup Parmesan cheese, grated
- 2 tablespoons olive oil

4 Servings   15 minutes

Directions

In a mixing bowl, thoroughly combine all the ingredients, except for the olive oil.

Shape the mixture into four equal patties.

Heat the olive oil in a frying pan over medium-high heat. Once hot, fry the patties for about 4 minutes per side or until golden browned.

Bon appétit!

Nutritional Information

Calories: 243; Fat: 16.5g; Carbs: 14.5g; Protein: 11.4g; Sugars: 4.2g; Fiber: 2.8g

21

13. Classic Mushroom Stroganoff

Ingredients

- 4 tablespoons olive oil
- 1 large onion, thinly sliced
- 2 large garlic cloves, crushed
- 2 pounds brown mushrooms, thinly sliced
- 1 teaspoon cayenne pepper
- Sea salt and ground black pepper, to taste
- 1 teaspoon thyme, chopped
- 1 teaspoon rosemary, chopped
- 1 bay leaf
- 1 cup heavy cream
- 2 cups water

4 Servings   25 minutes

Directions

Heat the olive oil in a stockpot over medium-high heat. Sauté the onion and mushrooms until they are softened and the mushrooms release liquid.

Now, stir in the garlic and continue to sauté for 2 minutes more or until they've softened.

Add in the remaining ingredients, except for the cream; stir to combine. Continue to simmer, partially covered, for about 20 minutes.

Fold in the cream and remove from the heat.

Bon appétit!

Nutritional Information

Calories: 272; Fat: 25.1g; Carbs: 9.4g; Protein: 4.9g; Sugars: 5.2g; Fiber: 2.2g

14. Roasted Cauliflower Chowder

Ingredients

- 1 pound cauliflower, cut into small florets
- 3 tablespoons olive oil
- 2 garlic cloves, chopped
- 1 celery stalk, chopped
- 1 bay leaf
- 1 thyme sprig, chopped
- 2 rosemary sprigs, chopped
- Kosher salt and freshly ground black pepper, to taste
- 4 cups vegetable broth
- 1/2 cup cheddar cheese, shredded
- 1 large egg, lightly whisked

5 Servings

55 minutes

Directions

Toss the cauliflower florets with 1 tablespoon of the olive oil. Roast the cauliflower florets in the preheated oven at 400 degrees F for about 22 minutes.

In a heavy-bottomed pot, heat the olive oil over medium-high flame. Sauté the garlic and celery until they are tender and fragrant.

Stir in the spices and broth. Add in the roasted cauliflower and stir to combine.

Pour in vegetable broth and bring to a boil. Turn the heat to medium-low and continue to simmer for 20 to 25 minutes.

Fold in the cheese and egg; stir to combine.

Continue to cook for 5 minutes more or until your chowder is thoroughly cooked. Enjoy!

Nutritional Information

Calories: 272; Fat: 25.1g; Carbs: 9.4g; Protein: 4.9g; Sugars: 5.3g; Fiber: 2.2g

Poultry

15. Easy Turkey Curry

Ingredients

- 1 tablespoon coconut oil
- 1 pound turkey breasts, diced
- 1 medium onion, thinly sliced
- 1 chili pepper, thinly sliced
- 2 cloves garlic, crushed or grated
- 1 teaspoon ginger, peeled and grated
- 2 teaspoons garam masala
- 1 tomato, pureed
- 1 cup coconut milk, unsweetened
- 1 cup vegetable broth
- Sea salt and ground black pepper, to taste

4 Servings   45 minutes

Directions

Heat the coconut oil in a saucepan. Once hot, brown the turkey for about 8 minutes or until it is golden brown.

Add in the onion, chili pepper, and garlic; continue to cook for a minute or so.

Add in the remaining ingredients. Continue to cook for about 35 minutes or until cooked through.

Serve warm and enjoy!

Nutritional Information

Calories: 272; Fat: 13.8g; Carbs: 6.4g; Protein: 28.8g; Sugars: 4.6g; Fiber: 0.6g

16. Spicy Herby Chicken Stew

Ingredients

- 2 tablespoons olive oil
- 2 pounds chicken thighs, cut into pieces
- 1 small onion, chopped
- 1 bell pepper, thinly sliced
- 2 garlic cloves, minced
- 1 chili pepper, thinly sliced
- Sea salt and ground black pepper, to taste
- 1/2 cup dry white wine
- 1/4 cup tomato paste
- 2 cups chicken broth
- 2 sprigs thyme, chopped
- 1 sprig rosemary, chopped
- 2 bay leaves

4 Servings

45 minutes

Directions

Heat the olive oil in a stockpot. Once hot, brown the chicken thighs for about 6 minutes or until no longer pink; reserve.

In the pan drippings, sauté the onion and bell pepper for 3 to 4 minutes or until they've softened.

Then, sauté the garlic and chili pepper for a minute or so.

Add in the remaining ingredients. Continue to cook for about 35 minutes or until cooked through.

Bon appétit!

Nutritional Information

26

Calories: 510; Fat: 20.7g; Carbs: 9.6g; Protein: 68.3g; Sugars: 4.6g; Fiber: 1.5g

17. Old-Fashioned Chicken Soup

Ingredients

- 3 teaspoons olive oil
- 1 large onion, chopped
- 4 cloves garlic, smashed
- 1 teaspoon fresh ginger, peeled and grated
- 1 chili pepper, seeded and chopped
- 1 medium carrot, peeled and chopped
- 1/2 pound cauliflower florets
- 1/2 teaspoon dried dill
- 1/2 teaspoon dried oregano
- 1/2 teaspoon crushed red pepper flakes
- Kosher salt and ground black pepper, to taste
- 4 cups chicken broth
- 1 stalk celery, thinly sliced
- 1 pound chicken breasts, skinless and boneless
- 2 tablespoons cilantro, chopped

4 Servings   30 minutes

Directions

Heat the olive oil in a heavy-bottomed pot over moderate flame. Cook the onion until they've softened.

Then, sauté the garlic, ginger, and chili pepper for about 1 minute or until tender and aromatic.

Add in the other ingredients and continue to simmer, partially covered, for a further 25 minutes. Bon appétit!

Nutritional Information

Calories: 314; Fat: 15.7g; Carbs: 9.4g; Protein: 31.3g; Sugars: 4.4g; Fiber: 2.5g

18. Easy Chicken Burger

Ingredients

- 1 pound ground chicken
- 2 ounces bacon, chopped
- 2 ounces Parmesan cheese, grated
- 1 small onion, chopped
- 2 cloves garlic, minced
- 1 egg, whisked
- 1/2 teaspoon dried oregano
- 1/4 teaspoon ground cumin
- 1/4 teaspoon ground cumin
- 1/2 teaspoon smoked paprika
- Kosher salt and ground black pepper, to taste
- 2 teaspoons olive oil
- 6 portobello mushrooms
- 6 lettuce leaves

3 Servings   20 minutes

Directions

Mix the chicken, bacon, cheese, onion, garlic, egg, and spices. Shape the mixture into patties.

Heat the olive oil in a frying pan over medium-high heat. Fry your patties for about 5 minutes per side.

Grill the portobello mushrooms for about 6 minutes or until cooked through.

Arrange your burgers with portobello buns, lettuce leaves, and patties. Enjoy!

Nutritional Information

Calories: 489; Fat: 31.8g; Carbs: 9.7g; Protein: 40.9g; Sugars: 5.4g; Fiber: 2.6g

19. Chicken Stew Olla Tapada

Ingredients

- 2 tablespoons olive oil
- 1 ½ pounds chicken drumsticks, boneless, skinless, cut small pieces
- 1 medium onion, chopped
- 1 medium bell pepper, trimmed and sliced
- 4 garlic cloves, chopped
- 1 chili pepper, seeded and chopped
- 4 cups chicken stock
- 1 tablespoon Mexican spice blend
- 2 tablespoons fresh parsley, chopped
- Sea salt and freshly ground black pepper, to taste

4 Servings

40 minutes

Directions

Heat the olive oil in a stockpot. Once hot, brown the chicken drumsticks for about 6 minutes or until no longer pink; reserve.

In the pan drippings, sauté the onion and bell pepper for 3 to 4 minutes or until they've softened.

Then, sauté the garlic and chili pepper for a minute or so.

Add in the remaining ingredients. Continue to cook for about 35 minutes or until cooked through.

Bon appétit!

Nutritional Information

Calories: 407; Fat: 24.7g; Carbs: 6.1g; Protein: 37.3g; Sugars: 2.4g; Fiber: 0.9g

20. Greek-Style Chicken Drumsticks

Ingredients

- 3 tablespoons olive oil
- 3 garlic cloves, minced
- 1 tablespoon balsamic vinegar
- 1 tablespoon freshly squeezed lemon juice
- 1 teaspoon dried oregano
- 1 teaspoon smoked paprika
- Kosher salt and freshly cracked black pepper, to taste
- 2 pounds chicken drumsticks, cut into pieces

5 Servings

50 minutes + marinating time

Directions

Whisk the olive oil, garlic, vinegar, lemon juice, and spices. Add in the chicken drumsticks and let them marinate for about 1 hour.

Preheat your oven to 420 degrees. Brush a baking pan with a nonstick cooking spray.

Arrange the marinated chicken on the baking pan; bake the chicken for about 45 minutes or until a meat thermometer registers 165 degrees F.

Bon appétit!

Nutritional Information

Calories: 407; Fat: 24.7g; Carbs: 6.1g; Protein: 37.4g; Sugars: 2.4g; Fiber: 0.9g

21. Creamed Chicken Salad

Ingredients

- 1 ½ pounds chicken breasts, skinless and boneless
- 1 cup mayonnaise
- 2 tablespoons cream cheese
- 1 teaspoon Dijon mustard
- 1 stalk celery, peeled and diced
- 2 green onions, sliced
- 1 small garlic clove, minced
- 1 bell pepper, chopped
- 2 tablespoon fresh parsley, chopped
- 1 tablespoon fresh tarragon, chopped
- Kosher salt and ground black pepper, to season

6 Servings

15 minutes + chilling time

Directions

Place the chicken breasts in a wide saucepan; cover by about 1 inch with water. Cook the chicken over medium heat for about 5 minutes.

Reduce the heat to low. Let the chicken simmer (covered) for a further 8 minutes or until the internal temperature reaches 165 degrees F.

Transfer the chicken to your refrigerator. Slice the chicken into bite-sized pieces. Add in the remaining ingredients.

Gently stir to combine and place your chicken in the refrigerator until ready to serve. Devour!

Nutritional Information

Calories: 467; Fat: 39.6g; Carbs: 2.3g; Protein: 24.4g; Sugars: 1.1g; Fiber: 0.3g

Meat

22. BBQ Pork Ribs

Ingredients

- Marinade:
- 1 teaspoon garlic, crushed
- 1 teaspoon onion powder
- 1 teaspoon smoked paprika
- Sea salt and freshly cracked black pepper, to taste
- 1/2 teaspoon cumin
- 1 bay laurel
- 1 thyme sprig
- 2 tablespoons olive oil
- BBQ Ribs:
- 2 pounds pork spare ribs
- 1 ½ cups barbecue sauce
- 1/2 cup red wine
- 2 tablespoons olive oil
- 2 tablespoons Worcestershire sauce

5 Servings   2 hours 15 minutes + marinating time

Directions

Mix all the marinade ingredients in a ceramic bowl. Add in the ribs and let them marinate for at least 2 hours.

Toss the ribs with the other ingredients.

Preheat your oven to 350 degrees F. Bake the ribs for 2 hours.

Next, place your ribs under the preheated broiler for about 10 minutes. Bon appétit!

Nutritional Information

Calories: 467; Fat: 39.6g; Carbs: 2.3g; Protein: 24.4g; Sugars: 1.1g; Fiber: 0.3g

23. Grandma's Beef Stew

Ingredients

- 2 tablespoons lard, melted
- 2 pounds beef shoulder, cut into cubes
- 1 large onion, thinly sliced
- 1 bell pepper, seeded and sliced
- 4 large garlic cloves, crushed
- 1 cup white wine
- 2 medium carrots, trimmed and sliced
- 3 cups chicken bone broth
- 2 bay leaves
- 1 teaspoon dried basil
- 1 thyme sprig
- 2 rosemary sprigs
- Sea salt and ground black pepper, to taste

5 Servings   50 minutes

Directions

In a heavy-bottomed pot, melt the lard until sizzling. Once hot, brown the beef for 4 to 5 minutes; season with salt and pepper and reserve.

Then, cook the onion and pepper for about 4 minutes or until they're just tender. Then, sauté the garlic for about 30 seconds or until aromatic. Add the remaining ingredients to the pot.

Partially cover and continue to simmer for about 40 minutes.

Bon appétit!

Nutritional Information

Calories: 372; Fat: 16.5g; Carbs: 4.2g; Protein: 24.4g; Sugars: 1g; Fiber: 7.2g

24. Hungarian-Style Pork Gulash

Ingredients

- 3 tablespoons olive oil
- 2 pounds pork roast, boneless and cut into bite-sized cubes
- 1 medium leek, chopped
- 1 bell pepper, chopped
- 3 garlic cloves, minced
- 1 chili pepper, chopped
- 2 carrots, peeled and cut into bite-sized chunks
- Kosher salt and ground black pepper, to taste
- 1 teaspoon Hungarian paprika
- 1/2 cup white wine
- 3 cups chicken bone broth
- 1 medium tomato, pureed
- 2 bay leaves

5 Servings   50 minutes

Directions

In a heavy-bottomed pot, heat the olive oil over medium-high heat. Once hot, brown the pork for 4 to 5 minutes; reserve.

Then, cook the leek and bell pepper for about 4 minutes or until they're just tender. Then, sauté the garlic and chili pepper for about 30 seconds or until aromatic.

Add the remaining ingredients, including the reserved pork, to the pot.

Partially cover and continue to simmer for about 40 minutes. Enjoy!

Nutritional Information

Calories: 444; Fat: 23.5g; Carbs: 9g; Protein: 43g; Sugars: 3.8g; Fiber: 1.8g

25. The Best Pork Patties Ever

Ingredients

- 1 ½ pounds ground pork
- 2 ounces bacon, chopped
- 2 cloves garlic, crushed
- Kosher salt and ground black pepper, to taste
- 1/2 teaspoon ground cumin
- 1 teaspoon cayenne pepper
- 1 tablespoon olive oil

5 Servings   15 minutes

Directions

Thoroughly combine all the ingredients, except for the olive oil. Shape the mixture into patties.

Heat the olive oil in a frying pan over medium-high heat. Fry your patties for about 5 minutes per side.

Enjoy!

Nutritional Information

Calories: 434; Fat: 36.2g; Carbs: 1.6g; Protein: 24.7g; Sugars: 0.6g; Fiber: 0.3g

26. Chunky Pork Frittata

Ingredients

- 1 tablespoon olive oil
- 1 pound ground pork
- 2 scallion stalks, chopped
- 1 garlic clove, chopped
- 1 Italian pepper, chopped
- 8 large eggs, lightly whisked
- 4 tablespoons Greek-style yogurt
- 2 tablespoons fresh basil leaves, chopped
- 2 tablespoons fresh parsley leaves, chopped
- Sea salt and ground black pepper, to taste
- 1 teaspoon cayenne pepper

4 Servings   35 minutes

Directions

Brush the sides and bottom of a baking pan with olive oil.

Mix all the ingredients until everything is well incorporated. Spoon the egg mixture into the baking pan.

Bake your frittata in the preheated oven at 360 degrees F for 30 minutes or until the eggs do not jiggle in the middle.

Devour!

Nutritional Information

Calories: 492; Fat: 37.2g; Carbs: 4.2g; Protein: 33.7g; Sugars: 2g; Fiber: 0.6g

27. Pork Souvlaki (Skewers)

Ingredients

- 1 ½ pounds pork shoulder, skinless, boneless and cut into bite-sized pieces
- 2 tablespoons soy sauce
- 2 tablespoons red wine
- 2 tablespoons extra-virgin olive oil
- 1 teaspoon dried Greek spice mix
- 1 teaspoon cayenne pepper
- Sea salt and ground black pepper, to taste

4 Servings

15 minutes + marinating time

Directions

Thoroughly combine all ingredients in a ceramic dish. Cover tightly and let it marinate in your refrigerator for 2 to 3 hours. Thread the pork cubes onto the skewers.

Prepare the outdoor grill and brush the grates with a nonstick cooking spray.

Grill your skewers until well browned and internal temperature registers 160 degrees F on an instant-read thermometer.

Bon appétit!

Nutritional Information

Calories: 369; Fat: 25.5g; Carbs: 2.3g; Protein: 30.3g; Sugars: 1.6g; Fiber: 0.3g

28. Old-Fashioned Pork Meatloaf

Ingredients

- 1 tablespoon lard
- 1 medium leek, finely chopped
- 2 garlic cloves, minced
- 1/2 pound ground pork
- 1/2 pound ground beef
- 2 ounces Parmesan cheese, grated
- 1 teaspoon dried marjoram
- 1/2 teaspoon cumin seeds
- Sea salt and ground black pepper, to taste
- 2 medium eggs, whisked
- 2 tablespoons soy sauce
- 1 tablespoon brown mustard
- 2 cups tomato puree

5 Servings   1 hour 5 minutes

Directions

Melt the lard in a frying pan over medium-high heat. Cook the leek and garlic until they have softened or about 3 minutes.

Add in the ground pork and cook until it is no longer pink, about 3 minutes. Add in the cheese, spices, and eggs.

Press the mixture into a loaf pan.

In a mixing bowl, whisk the soy sauce, mustard, and tomato puree. Spread the tomato glaze over the meatloaf.

Bake the meatloaf at 390 degrees F for about 55 minutes. Bon appétit!

Nutritional Information

Calories: 451; Fat: 33.3g; Carbs: 8.9g; Protein: 27.3g; Sugars: 2.9g; Fiber: 1.5g

29. Chinese Beef Stir Fry

Ingredients

- 2 tablespoons sesame oil
- 1 ½ pounds beef loin, slice into strips
- 2 tablespoons reduced-sodium soy sauce
- 2 tablespoons balsamic vinegar
- 1 red chili pepper, seeded and chopped
- 2 cloves garlic, minced
- 1 teaspoon fresh ginger, peeled and grated
- 1 small onion, thinly sliced
- 1 bell pepper, thinly sliced
- 1 cup broccoli florets

4 Servings   15 minutes

Directions

Heat sesame oil in a wok or large skillet.

Once hot, stir fry the beef for about 4 minutes.

Add in the remaining ingredients and stir fry for 5 to 6 minutes more. Devour!

Nutritional Information

Calories: 321; Fat: 14.3g; Carbs: 7.2g; Protein: 38.3g; Sugars: 3.5g; Fiber: 1.3g

Fish & Seafood

30. Spicy Halibut Salad

Ingredients

- 2 pounds halibut steak
- 4 tablespoons extra-virgin olive oil
- Kosher salt and ground black pepper, to taste
- 1 large red onion, thinly sliced
- 1 bell pepper, sliced
- 1 small chili pepper, seeded and sliced
- 1 garlic clove, minced
- 2 tablespoons fresh dill, chopped
- 2 tablespoons fresh lemon juice
- 2 tablespoons white wine vinegar
- 1 tablespoon capers, drained
- 1 tablespoon Dijon mustard
- 2 handfuls lettuce

5 Servings   **15 minutes**

Directions

Cook the halibut steak on preheated grill (or grill pan) for 5 to 6 minutes per side or until the fish flakes easily with a fork.

Slice the fish into strips. Add in the other ingredients,

Toss to combine; serve at room temperature or well-chilled. Enjoy!

Nutritional Information

Calories: 469; Fat: 36.3g; Carbs: 7.5g; Protein: 27.7g; Sugars: 2.7g; Fiber: 1.9g

31. Thai-Style Fish Curry

Ingredients

- 2 tablespoons coconut oil
- 1 medium onion, chopped
- 2 cloves garlic, chopped
- 1 teaspoon fresh ginger, peeled and grated
- 1 small chili pepper, chopped
- 2 teaspoons curry paste
- 1 teaspoon turmeric powder
- 1 cup milk
- 1 cup chicken bone broth
- 1 large tomatoes, pureed
- Sea salt and ground black pepper, to taste
- 1 teaspoon smoked paprika
- 1 ½ pounds codfish, cut into bite-sized chunks
- 2 tablespoons fresh coriander, roughly chopped
- 2 tablespoons freshly squeezed lime

4 Servings   25 minutes

Directions

Heat the oil in a saucepan over a moderate flame. Cook the onion until it has softened or about 4 minutes.

After that, sauté the garlic, ginger, and chili for about 1 minute or until fragrant.

Add in the remaining ingredients, except for the coconut milk, simmer for 10 minutes or until heated through.

Now, stir in the fish; pour in 1 cup of coconut milk and cook, covered, for 6 minutes longer.

Bon appétit!

Nutritional Information

Calories: 229; Fat: 8.3g; Carbs: 8g; Protein: 30.1g; Sugars: 5.4g; Fiber: 1.1g

32. Italian-Style Seafood Stew

Ingredients

- 2 tablespoons butter, softened
- 1 large leek, thinly sliced
- 2 large garlic cloves, minced
- 1 large tomatoes, pureed
- 1 ½ cups chicken bone broth
- 1/2 cup dry white wine
- 2 thyme sprigs
- 1 rosemary sprig
- 2 bay leaves
- 1 teaspoon hot sauce
- 1 tablespoon Italian herb mix
- Kosher salt and ground black pepper, to season
- 1 pound snapper fillets, cut into bite-sized chunks
- 1/2 pound scallops, deveined
- 2 tablespoons fresh Italian parsley, chopped

4 Servings   20 minutes

Directions

Melt the butter in a large pot over a moderately high heat. Sauté the leek and garlic until they've softened.

Stir in the pureed tomatoes and continue to cook for about 10 minutes.

Add in the remaining ingredients and bring to a boil. Immediately turn the heat to a simmer and continue to cook for 4 to 5 minutes.

Bon appétit!

Nutritional Information

44

Calories: 279; Fat: 8.3g; Carbs: 6.6g; Protein: 37.4g; Sugars: 2.4g; Fiber: 1g

33. Spicy Sea Bass Soup

Ingredients

- 2 tablespoons butter
- 1 medium onion, chopped
- 1 medium carrot, sliced
- 1 red bell pepper, chopped
- 2 garlic cloves, minced
- 1 teaspoon coriander
- 1/2 teaspoon ground cumin
- 1 teaspoon Aleppo pepper flakes
- 1 teaspoon turmeric powder
- 1 teaspoon smoked paprika
- 1 ½ pounds moderately sea bass, cut into bite-sized chunks
- Sea salt and ground black pepper, to taste
- 1 large tomato, pureed
- 1/2 cup dry white wine
- 3 cups chicken broth

4 Servings   20 minutes

Directions

Warm the butter in a soup pot over a moderately high flame. Cook the vegetables until they're softened.

Stir in the remaining ingredients. Bring to a boil.

Reduce the heat and partially cover the pot; continue to simmer your soup for 15 minutes longer or until cooked through. Bon appétit!

Nutritional Information

Calories: 299; Fat: 10.4g; Carbs: 7.6g; Protein: 36.1g; Sugars: 3.6g; Fiber: 1.6g

34. Baked Tilapia Fillets

Ingredients

- 1 pound tilapia fillets, about 3/4 inch thick
- 2 tablespoons extra-virgin olive oil
- 1 tablespoon lemon juice
- 4 ounces Parmesan cheese, grated
- 1 teaspoon garlic powder
- 1/2 teaspoon dried dill weed
- 1/2 teaspoon dried oregano
- 1 teaspoon dried parsley flakes
- Sea salt and ground black pepper, to taste
- 1/2 teaspoon hot paprika

4 Servings   20 minutes

Directions

Pat the fish dry and toss it with olive oil and lemon juice.

In a shallow bowl, mix all the remaining ingredients. Press the fish fillets onto the Parmesan mixture.

Bake the fish in the preheated oven at 375 degrees F for about 20 minutes or until the fish flakes easily with a fork.

Bon appétit!

Nutritional Information

Calories: 299; Fat: 10.4g; Carbs: 7.6g; Protein: 36.1g; Sugars: 3.6g; Fiber: 1.6g

35. Herbed Halibut Steaks

Ingredients

- 1 pound halibut steaks, 1-inch thick
- 2 tablespoons lime juice
- 2 tablespoons extra-virgin olive oil
- Kosher salt and ground black pepper, to taste
- 2 sprigs thyme, chopped
- 1 sprig rosemary, chopped
- 2 garlic cloves, crushed
- 2 tablespoons capers, drained

3 Servings   45 minutes

Directions

Place the halibut steaks along with the other ingredients in a ceramic dish; let it marinate for about 30 minutes.

Grill the halibut steaks approximately 15 minutes, turning occasionally and basting with the reserved marinade.

Bon appétit!

Nutritional Information

Calories: 330; Fat: 25.4g; Carbs: 3.2g; Protein: 22.3g; Sugars: 0.9g; Fiber: 0.6g

36. Fried Buttery Shrimp with Herbs

Ingredients

- 3 tablespoons butter
- 3 cloves garlic, minced
- 1 ½ pounds shrimp, peeled and deveined
- Sea salt and ground black pepper, to season
- 2 tablespoons fresh lime juice
- 4 tablespoons dry white wine
- 2 tablespoons fresh parsley, chopped
- 2 tablespoons fresh basil, chopped
- 1 tablespoon fresh mint, chopped

4 Servings

15 minutes

Directions

Melt the butter in a large skillet (or wok) over medium-high heat. Once hot, sauté the garlic until fragrant or approximately 1 minute.

Add in the shrimp, followed by the salt, black pepper, lime juice, and wine. Continue to cook for about 5 minutes or until they beginning to turn pink.

Garnish the fried shrimp with freshly chopped herbs and serve immediately.

Bon appétit!

Nutritional Information

48   Calories: 245; Fat: 9.6g; Carbs: 2.9g; Protein: 34.3g; Sugars: 0.9g; Fiber: 0.3g

Snacks & Appetizers

37. Cheesecake Fat Bombs

Ingredients

- 9 ounces cream cheese, room temperature
- 3 ounces coconut oil, softened
- 4 ounces double cream
- 1/4 teaspoon ground cinnamon
- 3 tablespoons erythritol
- 2 ounces coconut shreds

6 Servings   15 minutes

Directions

Thoroughly combine the cream cheese, coconut oil, cream, cinnamon, and erythritol.

Roll the mixture into small balls. Roll the balls onto the coconut shreds.

Bon appétit!

Nutritional Information

Calories: 365; Fat: 38.6g; Carbs: 3.7g; Protein: 3.3g; Sugars: 2.4g; Fiber: 0.9g

38. Parmesan Cauliflower Bites

Ingredients

- 1 pound cauliflower florets
- 1/2 teaspoon onion powder
- 1 teaspoon garlic powder
- 1/2 teaspoon dried dill weed
- Kosher salt and freshly ground black pepper, to taste
- 4 tablespoons olive oil
- 1/2 teaspoon hot sauce
- 1 cup Parmesan cheese, grated

4 Servings

45 minutes

Directions

Toss the cauliflower with spices, olive oil, and hot sauce.

Place the cauliflower florets on a parchment-lined baking pan.

Roast them in the preheated oven at 420 degrees F for about 35 minutes.

Toss the cauliflower with Parmesan cheese and continue to bake for a further 10 minutes. Enjoy!

Nutritional Information

Calories: 255; Fat: 20.8g; Carbs: 9.1g; Protein: 9.3g; Sugars: 2.2g; Fiber: 2.3g

39. Amish-Style Pickled Eggs

Ingredients

- 10 medium eggs
- 2 cloves garlic
- 2 ½ cups white vinegar
- 1 cup water
- 2 bay leaves
- 2 sprigs fresh dill
- 3 cardamom pods
- 1 tablespoon yellow curry powder
- 1 teaspoon yellow mustard seeds
- 1 teaspoon sea salt
- 1 medium onion, thinly sliced

5 Servings   15 minutes

Directions

Boil the eggs until hard-cooked; peel them and rinse under cold, running water. Add the peeled eggs to a large-sized jar.

Add all the remaining ingredients to a pan that is preheated over a moderately high heat; bring to a rapid boil.

Now, turn the heat to medium-low; let it simmer for 6 minutes. Pour the liquid over the eggs and seal the jar.

Refrigerate at least 3 days before serving. Bon appétit!

Nutritional Information

Calories: 158; Fat: 8.8g; Carbs: 3.1g; Protein: 11.3g; Sugars: 0.9g; Fiber: 0.8g

40. Italian-Style Dip

Ingredients

- 10 ounces cream cheese, room temperature
- 1 cup Mozzarella cheese, shredded
- 1 cup Provolone cheese, shredded
- 1 cup marinara sauce, no sugar added
- 1 tablespoon Italian spice mix
- 12 pepperoni slices
- 12 black olives, pitted

7 Servings   20 minutes

Directions

Begin by preheating your oven to 365 degrees F. Brush the sides and bottom of a baking pan with nonstick oil.

Thoroughly combine the cheese, marinara sauce, and spices. Place the mixture in the prepared baking dish.

Top with the pepperoni and olives and bake for 15 to 18 minutes or until hot and bubbly on top.

Bon appétit!

Nutritional Information

Calories: 266; Fat: 21.1g; Carbs: 5.1g; Protein: 13.7g; Sugars: 3.1g; Fiber: 1.1g

41. Greek-Style Deviled Eggs

Ingredients

- 10 large eggs
- 4 tablespoons Greek-style yogurt
- 5 tablespoons mayonnaise
- 1 teaspoon white vinegar
- 1 teaspoon yellow mustard
- 1 garlic clove, chopped
- Sea salt and ground black pepper, to taste
- 1 teaspoon dried oregano
- 2 tablespoons Kalamata olives, pitted and chopped
- 1 tablespoon fresh dill, chopped

5 Servings   **20 minutes**

Directions

Cook the eggs in a small saucepan and bring to a boil. Remove from the heat and let it stand, covered, for about 10 minutes.

Then, carefully peel the eggs.

Slice each egg in half lengthwise and remove the yolks. Thoroughly combine the yolks with Greek yogurt, mayo, vinegar, mustard, garlic, salt, black pepper, and oregano.

Divide the mixture among the egg whites. Top the eggs with olives and fresh parsley. Devour!

Nutritional Information

Calories: 256; Fat: 20.3g; Carbs: 2.7g; Protein: 14.3g; Sugars: 1.3g; Fiber: 0.4g

42. Bacon Asparagus Roll-Ups

Ingredients

- 12 thin asparagus spears, trimmed
- Coarse sea salt and black pepper, to season
- 1/2 teaspoon dried dill weed
- 1 teaspoon garlic powder
- 1 teaspoon onion powder
- 12 (1-ounce) slices pancetta

4 Servings

20 minutes

Directions

Toss your asparagus with salt, black pepper, cayenne pepper, dill, garlic powder, and onion powder. Place them on a parchment-lined baking sheet.

Bake your asparagus in the preheated oven at 420 degrees F for about 15 minutes; toss them halfway through the cooking time.

Roll the roasted asparagus spears in bacon and serve immediately!

Nutritional Information

Calories: 352; Fat: 33.4g; Carbs: 2.2g; Protein: 11.2g; Sugars: 0.9g; Fiber: 0.4g

43. Mini Cocktail Wieners

Ingredients

- 1 pound mini cocktail sausages
- 2 cups barbecue sauce, no sugar added
- 1 tablespoon Erythritol
- 1 teaspoon granulated garlic
- 2 tablespoons deli mustard

6 Servings   2 hours 5 minutes

Directions

Sear the sausage in a preheated nonstick skillet for 3 to 4 minutes. Place all ingredients in your slow cooker.

Cook on the Low setting for 2 hours. Serve with cocktail sticks or toothpicks.

Enjoy!

Nutritional Information

Calories: 292; Fat: 24g; Carbs: 6.6g; Protein: 12.2g; Sugars: 3.4g; Fiber: 1.8g

Desserts

44. Chocolate Almond Candy

Ingredients

- 9 ounces dark chocolate chunks, no sugar added
- 1/2 cup double cream
- 2 ounces cream cheese, room temperature
- 1 teaspoon vanilla extract
- 1/2 teaspoon almond extract
- 1/4 teaspoon grated nutmeg
- 1/4 teaspoon cinnamon
- 2 ounces almonds, chopped

10 Servings   **10 minutes**

Directions

Microwave the chocolate chunks; add in the cream, cheese, and spices. Roll the mixture into equal balls.

Roll the balls over the chopped almonds until well coated.

Bon appétit!

Nutritional Information

Calories: 239; Fat: 20.4g; Carbs: 9g; Protein: 5.3g; Sugars: 0.8g; Fiber: 5.1g

45. Almond and Ginger Cheesecake

Ingredients

- 1/2 cup almond meal
- 2 tablespoons coconut oil
- 1 teaspoon ginger, peeled and grated
- 20 ounces cream cheese
- 1 ½ cups full-fat yogurt
- 2/3 cup erythritol
- 1 tablespoon fresh lemon juice
- 1/4 teaspoon anise, ground
- 1 teaspoon pure vanilla extract

8 Servings   25 minutes

Directions

Begin by preheating your oven at 350 degrees F. Line a baking pan with a parchment paper.

Thoroughly combine the almond meal, coconut oil, and ginger. Press the crust into the baking pan.

Beat the remaining ingredients using your electric mixer on high speed. Spoon the mixture over the crust.

Bake your cheesecake for about 20 minutes. Enjoy!

Nutritional Information

Calories: 337; Fat: 31.4g; Carbs: 7.9g; Protein: 7.8g; Sugars: 5.8g; Fiber: 0.8g

46. Classic Fudge Bites

Ingredients

- 1 cup butter, room temperature
- 1/2 cup cream cheese
- 1/2 cup cocoa powder, unsweetened
- 1/4 cup almond meal
- 1 tablespoon powdered monk fruit
- 1/4 teaspoon ground cinnamon
- A pinch of grated nutmeg

9 Servings

10 minutes +
chilling time

Directions

Thoroughly combine all the ingredients in a bowl until well combined.

Drop by teaspoonfuls onto foil-lined baking sheets. Chill the fudge bites in your refrigerator until firm.

Bon appétit!

Nutritional Information

Calories: 251; Fat: 26.4g; Carbs: 3.9g; Protein: 2.4g; Sugars: 0.6g; Fiber: 1.8g

47. Chocolate Almond Squares

Ingredients

- 2 cups dark chocolate chunks, no sugar added
- 4 tablespoons almond butter
- 1 cup double cream
- 1 teaspoon vanilla extract
- 1/4 cup flaxseed meal
- 1/2 cup almonds, chopped

10 Servings

10 minutes +
chilling time

Directions

Thoroughly combine all the ingredients in a mixing bowl.

Spoon the batter into the bottom of a parchment-lined baking pan.

Place the baking pan in the refrigerator for about 1 hour. Cut your cake into squares and enjoy!

Nutritional Information

Calories: 277; Fat: 24.5g; Carbs: 9.1g; Protein: 4.8g; Sugars: 0.6g; Fiber: 5.5g

48. Kid-Friendly Chocolate Cupcakes

Ingredients

- Cupcakes:
- 1 cup almond meal
- 1/4 cup flaxseed meal
- 1 teaspoon baking powder
- 1/4 cup cocoa powder
- 1/2 teaspoon ground cinnamon
- A pinch of grated nutmeg
- A pinch of sea salt
- 4 tablespoons monk fruit powder
- 1/4 cup full-fat coconut milk
- 2 eggs
- Frosting:
- 1/2 cup butter, softened
- 1/2 cup heavy cream
- 4 tablespoons monk fruit powder
- 1 teaspoon pure vanilla extract

10 Servings

20 minutes + chilling time

Directions

Start by preheating your oven to 350 degrees F. Brush a muffin tin with nonstick oil.

Stir the dry ingredients for the cupcakes until well combined. Stir in the remaining ingredients for the cupcakes; mix to combine well.

Spoon the mixture into the prepared muffin tin.

Bake your cupcakes in the preheated oven for about 13 minutes or until a tester comes out dry.

Meanwhile, using an electric mixer, beat all the frosting ingredients until fluffy.

Frost your cupcakes and serve well-chilled! Devour!

Nutritional Information

Calories: 199; Fat: 18.9g; Carbs: 5.5g; Protein: 4.8g; Sugars: 1g; Fiber: 3.1g

49. Vanilla Chia Pudding

Ingredients

- 4 tablespoons chia seeds
- 1 cup full-fat coconut milk
- 1 cup water
- 2 tablespoons coconut oil
- 1/2 teaspoon pure vanilla extract
- 1/4 teaspoon ground cinnamon
- 1/4 teaspoon ground cloves
- A few stevia drops

2 Servings   30 minutes

Directions

Place all the ingredients in two serving bowls.

Allow them to stand for about 30 minutes, stirring periodically.

Bon appétit!

Nutritional Information

Calories: 269; Fat: 22.2g; Carbs: 9.3g; Protein: 6.3g; Sugars: 6.2g; Fiber: 5.2g

50. Avocado Cheesecake Mousse

Ingredients

- 1 large ripe avocado
- 2 tablespoons fresh lime juice
- 4 ounces cream cheese, room temperature
- A pinch of kosher salt
- A pinch of grated nutmeg

4 Servings **10 minutes**

Directions

Thoroughly combine all the ingredients in your blender or a food processor.

Mix until creamy, smooth and uniform.

Enjoy!

Nutritional Information

Calories: 312; Fat: 29.8g; Carbs: 9.4g; Protein: 4.7g; Sugars: 2.2g; Fiber: 4.7g

www.ingramcontent.com/pod-product-compliance
Lightning Source LLC
Chambersburg PA
CBHW081545040426
42448CB00015B/3233